The Murray-Darling River, Darling:

A take on Australia's Murray-Darling River

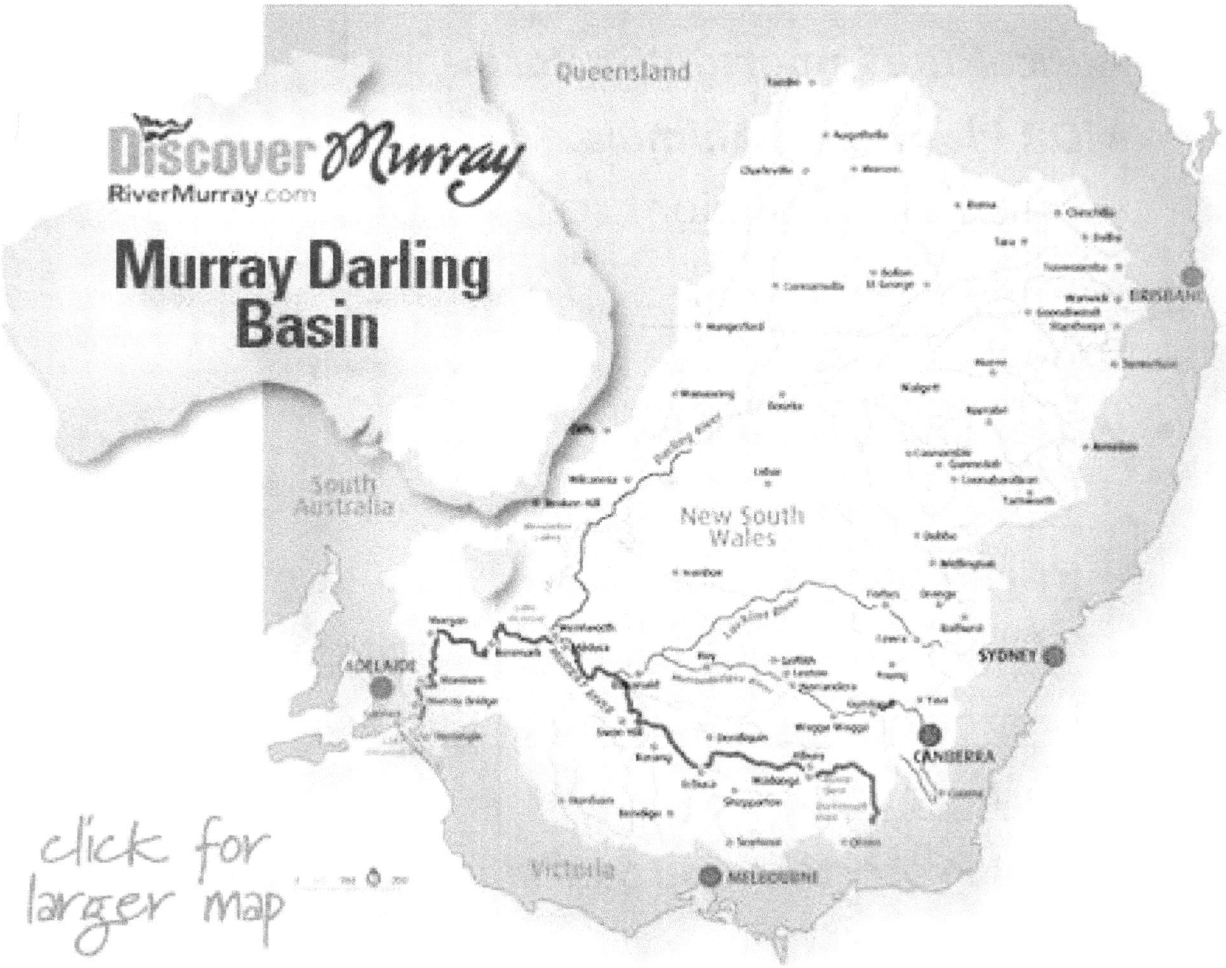

The Murray-Darling River, Darling:

A take on Australia's Murray-Darling River

Contents

1. Introduction
2. Themes/Subjects:
- *Condition of Basin*
- *History of the MDRB*
- *Archaeology and Geography of MDRB*
- *Agriculture important in Basin*
- *MDR Plants and Animals*
  - Human introduction
- *Climate Change*
  Drought
- *Water and the MDRB*
  - Water Usage
  - Irrigated Crops
  - Water Conveyancing/Transportation
  - Improving Water Catchment areas
  - Desalination
- *MDRB Protection and Sustainability*
- *Government*

- *MDRB Farmers like others with a business*
- *Networking companies, farming and health and fitness boom*
3. Conclusion

1. Introduction

The Murray-Darling River Basin (MDRB) is one of Australia's largest rivers. It is made up of three rivers, creeks and watercourses – The Darling River, The Murray River and the Murrumbidgee River (Murray-Darling Basin). The world is predominantly made up of water through the oceans – "97% of the world's water is contained in the oceans as saltwater…0.15% in rivers [e.g. MDRB], streams, lakes and atmosphere" (The Murray Darling Basin). The MDRB holds great significance for Australia and the world because it has many areas to provide for. MDRB provides a staggering "14% of total area of Australia", or "1,062,025km2 or "one-seventh of the total area of mainland Australia" (The Murray-Darling Basin). MDRB is made up of a "total of 23 river valleys" (The Murray Darling Basin). A number of states are a part of the MDRB, with "Victoria, New South Wales, South Australia, Queensland and the ACT" (The Murray-Darling River). It is said that "over 2 million people live in the Basin (The Murray-Darling Basin)." The Basin is going to cost an estimated "$12 billion dollars or more this decade" (Sturmer, J. & Harmsen, N. 12 October, 2015).

The River provides considerable food from farming and agriculture and encompasses many animal, plant and ecosystems species and water resources. However, the Basin is under attack from forces such as climate change, drought and water shortage, animal and plant endangerment and extinction sustainable land management and reduced funding.

1. Subjects/Themes

Condition of Basin

Currently, inflows into the MDR system are now as low as they were in 2002-2003, [and 2006-to-2009 even worse], which was the "first bad year for what is called the 'Millennium Drought', " according to David Dreveman, MDR's executive director of river management. In 2002, inflows were the "Basin's fifth-lowest and driest year on record...the water stored in dams/storages [like Dartmouth and Hume and South Australia] could only stretch so far...they [dams/storages] can't protect you year after year" (ABC Rural, October 23, 2015)." The government's "Sustainable Rivers Audit", was "the most comprehensive assessment of the health of the MDRB ever undertaken." The Audit found that "21 of the 23 valleys in the MDRB were in a poor, very poor or extremely poor condition (Sturmer, J. and Harmsen, N. 12 October 2015)."

Vidot highlights how "in September 2015 there was 490 gigalitres of inflow into the MDRB, whilst in 2006 it was only 125 gigalitres of inflow for the September. However, parties involved in the MDRB are "a lot better positioned to deal with the MDRB's conditions than a decade ago (Vidot, A. 23 October, 2015)."

History of the MDRB

The resources of the Basin were used by European settlement whom had water and agricultural needs. During this time of early European settlement, there was little understanding of the needs of the MDRB natural environment. This lack of understanding lead to over-use and over-consumption of MDRB resources, contributing to the decline of the MDRB, along with "drought, decreasing river flows and increasing salinity (Murray-Darling Basin Authority)."

Archaeology and Geography of MDRB

The Murray-Darling River Basin (MDRB) "is a large geographical region in the interior of southeastern Australia." MDRB is "one-seventh of the Australian land mass" and is "flat, low-lying and far inland (Wikipedia – Murray-Darling Basin)."

The Basin is an extraordinary "350 million-years-old". Over this time, ancient underlying rock was made and took shape. Rising sea levels put salty sediments, forming river plains. Water collected in these layers of sand and clay, formed valuable, inland underground water sources. An example is the southern-eastern highlands of Australia, which was made 32 to 65 million years ago, almost back to the Dinosaur period. This has made the MDRB "relatively flat, being only 200 metres above sea level...and making many twists and turns, over plains...having low contact with other rivers, on the way to the ocean" (Murray-Darling Basin Authority).

Some examples of the Basin's natural, cultural, archaeological and geological sites are: " 'Lake Victoria', where thousands of Aboriginal burial grounds have been discovered;" " 'Lightning Ridge', which had 125-million-year-old fossils of platypus ancestors;" and " 'Willandra Lakes World Heritage Area', with sites of the world's oldest-known human cremations of Mungo Women and Mungo Man" (Murray-Darling Basin Authority).

Agriculture important in Basin

The Basin agricultural production is important in that it accounts for a huge "39% of the national economy income, or total gross value." MDRB produces "one third of Australia's food supply". MDRB includes "40% of all Australian farms" and makes "three quarters of Australia's irrigated crops and pastures". It produces the raw materials for most of the Basin's manufacturing and processing activities. There are "about 3.5% (200,000) of Australia's workforce employed in agriculture, with more workers in the Basin (Murray-Darling Basin).

MDRB produces "wool, cotton, wheat, sheep, cattle, dairy produce, rice, oil-seed, wine, fruit and vegetables for both domestic and overseas markets." MDR produces "53% of Australian cereals [barley, oats, cereal rye, buckwheat, triticale and wheat] grown for grain, 95% of oranges and 54% of apples." Meat enterprises dominate Basin agriculture, especially in the western and southern

Basins. The Basin looks after most, or a large proportion of Rice and Cotton production. Dairy is more prevalent in the northeast and north-central Victoria and Southern NSW in the Murray catchment. The MDRB supports "28% of the nation's cattle herd, 45% of sheep and 62% of pigs." There are also "poultry, goats, deer, bees, ostriches, alpacas and horses." (The Murray-Darling Basin).

MDR Plants and Animals

The MDR Basin is home to a large variety of different plants and animals and ecosystems, with some, if not more, extinct or endangered. According to the Murray-Darling Basin, there are "80 species of mammals, 55 species of frogs, 46 species of snakes, five species of tortoises, 35 endangered species of birds, 16 species of endangered mammals, over 35 different native fish species...and 20 species of mammals that have become extinct." Many of "these native plants and animals belong to, and are protected in national parks and other reserves which cover about 7 percent of the Basin's total area...and part of 30,000 wetlands" (Murray-Darling Basin). Examples are the "Darling Lily flower...Bogong

Moth...Australian Pelican...Imperial White Butterfly...Corroboree Frog...Cane Toad...and Murray Cod." Pastures for grazing and production have many introduced plants, such as "subterranean clovers, annual medics, serradella and lucerne" (Murray-Darling Basin).

Human introduction

Various people and populations using the Murray-Darling River Basin (MDRB) have affected the region with use of these plant and animal species, for good and bad. An example of this is the number of recreational activities of the wetlands, and 'anglers' – "human introduction, possibly by anglers using smaller carp illegally as live bait has also increased their [Carps] distribution...Carp are a problem in that they feed by sucking gravel from the river bed and take all the edible material off it (Wikipedia – Murray-Darling Basin)."

Climate Change

It is interesting to note that the Murray-Darling Basin (MDRB) "has a big variety of climatic conditions, with generally dry, but highly variable climate (The Murray Darling Basin/ Murray-Darling Basin Authority)." It is said that MDRB has "highly diverse landscapes, ranging from sub-tropical conditions in the far north, cool hurried eastern uplands, high alpine country of the Snowy Mountains, the temperate south-east, to the hot and dry semi-arid and arid western plains (The Murray Darling Basin)." The number of climatic conditions across the Basin means "there is a whole range of agricultural commodities being produced (Murray-Darling Basin)." An example of climate change is the growth and strength of the 'El Nino' affect in the Pacific. The Bureau of Meteorology states that the "current El Nino will intensify to record levels by Christmas [2015] and continue well into next year (Vidot, A. 23 October, 2015)."

Drought

The 2001 Agricultural Census stated that drought conditions in the Murray-Darling River Basin (MDRB) have been occurring for the last decade, especially since 1995. Vidot states how "lakes are only 5% full now, and the largest [lake], Lake Menindee, is bone dry (Vidot, A. 23 October, 2015)." As a result, there has been reduced production output and less income for agricultural enterprises. Some MDRB communities state they are "living in a man-made drought because of government buybacks and the Basin Plan", with these actions supposed to help, not burden, the MDRB and its people (ABC Rural, October 23, 2015). With Wetlands for example, "during drought, they provide refuges for wildlife and grazing stock" (Murray-Darling Basin Authority). The drought and water crisis "has changed the way water resources are managed and allocated in the MDRB (Vidot, A. 23 October, 2015).

Water and the MDRB

Water Usage

The MDRB's "most valuable resource is 'water' (Murray-Darling Basin)." The MDRB area provides a very small percentage of water, "mainly along the southern and eastern rims." There is very little or no regular water supply to the MDRB from the almost "86% of the vast catchment area". The MDRB "annual average rainfall is 530,618 gigalitres (GL). The "94% of rainfall evaporates, 2% drains into the ground and 4% ends up as runoff (Murray-Darling Basin)." The government has allocated $10 billion to return water to the environment. This money will set the stage for the sharing of water supplies for farmers and relevant parties in the MDRB (Vidot, A. 23 October, 2015). There looks to be what is called a 'carryover', to store left over farmers' unused and unneeded water until the following year or next usage (Vidot, A. 23 October, 2015). The NSW Government will recently look to spend $500 million on a proposed water pipeline from the Murray River to Broken Hill in NSW's far west, to fix the region's water supply problem (Gooch, D. and Glanville, B. June 16, 2016).

Irrigated Crops

Plants and animals and ecosystems of the MDRB need water supply. " 'Agricultural Irrigation' accounts for about 95% of water removed from the MDRB." There is an emphasis on the large amount of water needed to grow food in the Basin and other areas. Different ways have been developed to conserve and improve water efficiency. An example of this the 'CSIRO Land and Water scientists'. It is amazing the skill and equipment and machinery used and needed by these scientists. The scientists "used precision weighing systems to measure water use by various crops, and the yield from the crops (Murray Darling Basin]."

The figures were "determined in very controlled conditions and varied with the environment and methods of water delivery and harvesting used." Examples of the measurements by these scientists were: to produce "one kilogram of oven dry wheat grain, it takes 715-750 litres of water; for 1kg of maize, 540 to 630 litres; for 1kg of paddy rice, 1550 litres; for 1kg of beef, 50,000 to 100,000 litres; and for 1kg of clean wool, 170,000 litres" (Murray-Darling Basin). Some foods respond better than others to water irrigation by the scientists. All that can be said is there is an absolute staggering amount of water needed by this MDRB agriculture and related items, and will definitely require effective and efficient planning and management. The Commonwealth and relevant parties of the Basin have also "invested millions of dollars of Commonwealth money to improve the water efficiency on irrigated farms" (Vidot, A. 23 October, 2015).

Water Conveyancing/Transportation

A problem exists where flora, fauna and wetlands can lose water usage. Irrigated or rain fed plants, animals and ecosystems can lose water by "transpiration, evaporation and seepage, even before it actually reaches the farm." A mammoth "85% of water can be lost, from river to farm gate, with the use of older-style 'open earthen channel supplies'. On the other hand, only 5% of water is lost when 'new fully piped systems are used' " (Murray-Darling Basin).

Improving Water Catchment areas

More needs to be done to catch and store water properly for the MDRB. A large 94% of rainfall is lost to evaporation. Something must be done to combat this poor statistic through better water catchment areas. The 2 million and over population of the MDRB can install more 'home water tanks' and use stored and recycled water for everyday use such as planting and gardening, pools and toilet use. The use of 'new fully piped systems', is one example of better water catchment, losing only a minute 5% compared to 85% lost from open earthen channel supplies.

Desalination

Due to the fact that 97% of the world's water, saltwater, is kept in the oceans, a strong idea is using this collosal water supply for the MDRB and, what is needed elsewhere. Archaeological and geological, and cultural and natural heritage sites, as in southern-eastern highlands for instance, and discussed previously, show heavy consolidation of sand and clay in the land. With some assigned method from farmers, scientists and government, the salt can be removed from the salty oceans of the world to produce clean, fresh water for irrigation and the like. Former Prime Minister and Liberal party leader, John Howard, had the idea and promise of 'Desalination'. This Desalination has only taken place to a minimal extent and so much more can be done.

With reduced water flows, "diesel-powered dredges", used on the 'Murray mouth' for example, aim to "stop enormous amounts of sand coming in", at "1,800 cubic metres a day." This dredging shows that more water is required (Sturmer, J. & Harmsen, N. 12 October, 2015).

MDRB Protection and Sustainability

Teamwork is need between farmers and their workers, the agricultural industry, business, educational institutions, scientists, government and general public to establish, improve and develop proper MDRB protection and sustainability. Obtaining profits for the MDRB is one important factor, but protection and sustainability is another significant issue. Scientists connected to the Basin state that "without adequate oversight, monitoring and evaluation of the [MDRB] system, governments are in fact blind to what is happening in the Basin" (Sturmer, J. & Harmsen, N. 12 October, 2015). Professor Kingsford, who operates the UNSW Centre for Ecosystem Science, made a submission to a Senate inquiry and highlighted the lack of proper monitoring of the MDRB and the Basin Plan. Only "10 million dollars" is spent by the government on monitoring and evaluation, or in other words, only "0.1% of total water reform expenditure" (Sturmer, J. & Harmsen, N. 12 October, 2015).

Like the early European settlers in Australia and with direct contact with the MDRB, people today have over-used and over-consumed the resources of the MDRB. A strong example of this is the attempted protection of the many native plants and animals, yet endangerment and extinction occurs (Murray-Darling Basin). The Murray-Darling Basin Commission (MDBC) "promotes the awareness of the need for changes to the management of the land and water resources of the Basin, such as salinity management, monitoring the health of the Basin rivers and ensuring proper distribution of water from the Murray-Darling (Wikipedia, 'Murray-Darling Basin)."

Government

MDR covers five state and territory governments, who under the Constitution, look after the MDRB and its water resources. Under the governments, the River Murray Commission (RMC) was created in 1917, also establishing the River Murray Waters Agreement. The RMC only had an advisory role, not an enforcement role of provisions for the MDRB. In 1982, water quality, on a national perspective, became part of the Commission's responsibilities, after salinity became an issue.

In stating this, the Murray-Darling Basin Agreement came in to play in 1985, but was not fully enacted until 1993. This Agreement enabled the creation of new organisations, with the Murray-Darling Basin Initiative, the Murray-Darling Basin Ministerial Council and Murray-Darling Basin Commission. The 'Murray-Darling Basin Plan' was put in place in November 2012-March 2013 by Minister Tony Burke, the Minister for Sustainability, Environment, Water, Population and Communities (Wikipedia, 'Murray-Darling Basin'). The months ahead in 2015 will be crucial to the success of the Basin Plan. There was also the use of the "Sustainable Rivers Audit" being carried out, as mentioned previously.

In relation to MDRB protection and sustainability, some farmers and politicians are teaming up to help farmers poor farming conditions - "An alliance of Victorian agricultural producers and crossbench senators are leading a push to change and reform how water is managed along the MDRB (Vidot, A. & Iggulden, T. 15 October, 2015)" Low rainfall and low water supply and drought have made current farming conditions a crisis. Lost crops have been given away as fodder by farmers. Mental health of farmers has also been an issue for a while.

Water Policy is now a hotly debated topic by farmers and relevant politicians. For example, newly appointed Prime Minister and Liberal leader, Malcolm Turnball has tried to calm tension over current water policy. Turnball will likely choose Agriculture Minister, Barnaby Joyce, who wants to re-open a possible comprehensive audit of the MDRB, which was axed by state governments three years ago, or Turnball's new assistant minister and South Australian Liberal senator, Anne Rustons, to take care of the water policy. Some think Senator Joyce might cause problems for the water policy and parties involved. However, Joyce was "Opposition Water Spokesman between 2010 and 20013" (Sturmer, J. & Harmsen, N. 12 October 2015). Additionally, it cannot be denied that Joyce has some understanding about agriculture and irrigation.

The main issue is freeing up the 'Commonwealth Environmental Water Holder (CEWH)' to allow to temporarily sell water allocations to farmers and or irrigators. The CEWH would work together with the MDR Basin Plan to monitor and enforce water policy and water rights. On the other hand, this is also a problem for farmer-irrigators in that water bought back will be sorely missed for their owns farms, being used for environmental use, with the term 'environmental' being a bit broad, open and reckless in a way related to water policy. This would create more animosity, lack of control and competition on the temporary market for farmers and government to have and use water.

The money of these sales of water can be re-invested in water-saving efficiency projects, hence a form of MDRB protection and sustainability, as mentioned previously. On the contrary, some farmers, as in Victoria for example, claim Commonwealth involvement in water policy has pushed water prices higher. An example of this was water trading at $300 per megalitre on temporary market compared to $1000 a megalitre in 2006-2007. Who can say that the government or farmers/agricultural parties do a better job with water policy. In stating this, some senators want the implementation of the MDR Basin Plan to be holted for a while until the full 'social and economic and environmental impacts' are truly and properly understood (Vidot, A. 23 October, 2015).

According to Vidot, some Murray irrigators have most reliable 'high security licenses', and will receive all the water they need and deserve. Vidot continues, with how less reliable 'general security licenses' of Murray irrigators will only get 12% of their water entitlements (Vidot, A. 23 October, 2015). This either exposes some bias and possible corruption or the fact some MDRB farmers, and some farmers in general, have more important and busier farms compared to other farmers.

MDRB Farmers like others with a business

There are some members of the Australian and overseas communities who are working and have their own businesses, and feel farmers should be treated like everyone else. In other words, no sympathy or understanding should be given for the MDRB and its farmers and their staff. This is in a way quite a harsh viewpoint by these people. MDRB farming and agriculture are a business, but they provide such an important and foundational resource with the food and goods the general public purchase. One can compare a supermarket to a standard store and view the amount of people needing everyday, non-durable goods like those provided by the MDRB compared to the durable items people buy now-and-again like clothes and white good (fridge and washing machine).

Networking companies, farming and health and fitness boom

Networking companies like Nutriway-Amway, GNLD and USANA all pride themselves on their good, solid supplements from top quality farming practices. This is also to build on booms in Wealth Creation and Health and Fitness. Nutriway for example has specialized farms in California and Mexico. Nutriway's farms use the best farming goods and practices and methods, with quality, natural organic good. One can tell the difference between properly farmed Networking produce and other goods. It could be said that MDRB farming is similar, in a way, to these Networking farms, in that, in general, and even to a greater degree, the MDRB provide enough quality farmed food and items.

Conclusion

The importance, impact and effects of the Murray-Darling River Basin (MDRB) in Australia cannot be denied. It is amazing how this area provides so much of agriculture and industry. There are a number of significant issues surrounding the Basin. Some of these issues are weather, drought and rainfall, climate change, funding, transportation, better farming methods and protection and sustainability of the region, among other issues. It is great to see improvement after improvement, with parties like the general public, business and government all, eventually, coming to the aid of the MDRB. As stated earlier, these next coming months in 2005 will be crucial to see what lies ahead for the MDRB. An example of this is the response, action and affects to the MDRB by new Liberal leader and now Prime Minister, Malcolm Turnball, and his new Cabinet.

Bibliography

- ABC Rural (23 October, 2015) 'Murray-Darling inflows on par with 2002: MDBA'

- Geoscience Australia (Australian Government), 'Longest Rivers'

- Gooch, Declan. and Glanville, Brigid. (June 16, 2016) 'Broken Hill water crisis: NSW to build Murray River pipeline under $500m supply plan', ABC News

- Murray-Darling Basin Authority, 'Basin Environment', 'Geology and Size', 'Rivers and wetlands of the Murray-Darling',

- The Murray-Darling Basin/Wetlands –
www.murraydarlingwetlands.com.au

- Murray Darling Basin –

www.murrayriver.com.au

- References:

Personal Experiences: - I was a member of Network 21 and Nutriway-Amway for 4-years.

- My cousin's husband is a Mutton/Lamb farmer.

- Sturmer, Jake. & Harmsen, Nick. (12 October, 2015) 'Barnaby Joyce looks to revive health audit of Murray-Darling Basin,' <u>ABC News</u>
- Vidot, Anne. (23 October, 2015) 'Water flows into Murray-Darling system now equal to 2002, fifth-driest year on record', <u>ABC Rural</u>
- Vidot, Anne. & Iggulden, T. (15 October, 2015) 'Crossbench senators, agricultural producers in alliance to change how Murray-Darling river system is managed', <u>ABC News</u>
- Wikipedia, 'Murray-Darling Basin'